I was raised in a house of water

juniper klatt

Fernwood
PRESS

I was raised in a house of water
©2019 by juniper klatt

Fernwood Press
Newberg, Oregon
www.fernwoodpress.com

All rights reserved. No part may be reproduced
for any commercial purpose by any method without
permission in writing from the copyright holder.

Printed in the United States of America

Cover design: Mareesa Fawver Moss

ISBN 978-1-59498-056-5

I was raised in a house of water is a gentle rainfall of words, each verse the soft whisper of an old friend, sharing their most patient observations, deepest longings, and wisest insights. "Yes, I am here in this world." I read these poems, inhaling each line as I travel; truly a space in between. "Hold space for an eternal moment," juniper writes, and I can't help but sense a deep wisdom in their words, connecting disparate places, times, and stories. "May we see one another. May we see ourselves." Wherever you find yourself on your journey, juniper invites you to go deeper, to listen, and to trust.

C. Wess Daniels
author of *A Convergent Model of Renewal*

Poems that touch more deeply, soothe more gently, and challenge more aggressively. juniper is one of the best in the Northwest because she is willing, not only to look within herself, but also to exist.

Julian Phillip Doumit
Little Comfort

juniper sings a song of experience—the sanctification and romance of life: "To shift is to be alive." Their words, drenched in the devastation of being, help us hold on to hope.

Hye Sung
Friendly Fire Collective

juniper klatt has more than succeeded in writing their life as a poem in this stunning collection. The naturalness of the work is easy like a comfy sweater, and as juniper removes one layer after another, they make it safe to approach hard truths and beautiful stories. At the end, juniper seems to stand naked before us, and you can do nothing else but join them.

M Jahntz

Beautiful words shared from a beautiful heart always.

Amy Kopsa

juniper expresses the beauty and challenge of our times. She speaks of love, loss, and cookie-baking. But the poem that best captures the joy of being a human being, and the one I'd most like to hear her read out loud, begins, "I forgot how to pray with the structured words of my teachers and preachers and remembered how to dance with the colors and moans and songs of my ancestors." juniper invites us to make magic. And to dance.

Stephen Deatherage

Aw well! She knows how to touch my soul to my toes. She's got a knack for articulating that connection oh so lovely. It's her gift for sure.

Lori Williams

juniper's ability to gather together the pieces of the world—her curation of the sensory and emotional—makes me pause. To wonder and wonder.

Damon Motz-Storey

We sat across from each other at a table many years ago. juniper looked like any other beautiful young woman just coming into her own. The next day, her time came to stand at the microphone, and as she began her heart performance, the depth and strength—the wisdom and power that came as she transformed into her poem—stunned me. I will never forget. juniper is a gift, for she can speak deeply what so many of us feel. I am grateful for her presence in the world.

Lori Bosteder

to the water signs who made me
to the loves & lovers who've held me
to every version of my self I am trying to love

this is how I feel the world

I was raised in a house of water

I'm sitting across the table from my
grandmother, the house sighs
in the silence, releasing a breath
held for generations
I look up into her smile-wrinkled
face, with my hand wrapped
around my mug of earl grey tea
even as her hand wraps
around her own mug
of earl grey

"Grandma," I say, "I miss you"
but what I mean to say, as
tears well in my blue green
eyes is, "I love you"
"thank you"
"I'm sorry"

We don't need words as the
space between us is filled with
the sweet honey and cookie-baking-
in-the-oven taste of
love beyond borders
beyond the divide of life and spirit
of death and being reborn

As I watch the steam rise
from our cups, mingling with
air and breath from our
lungs like a dance
the empty chairs at the table
begin to have a
presence, and the
room fills up on the
edges, with the living
and the dead

"Hello mom," and though
uncharacteristically she is
quiet, her smile warms the
room like sunshine
and we are all bathed
in her light

My nana Mary comes in through
the kitchen, smelling of roses
with a fabulous scarf wrapped
about her like she is ready
for a show. And maybe she is

But she doesn't sing, this
time. She opens her heart like
a flower and the sweetness
of her presence holds the
room in beauty

My grandmother sips her
tea—the ground, the earth
the rock beneath our feet
and creaky wooden chair legs
She is the sustainer, the
maker, the space creator
and as she breathes, we all
relax and breathe into
ourselves

We wait in the quiet chill of
the morning, while silently
the spaces in-between words and
emptiness find themselves alive
with the spirits of those
connected to us, woven into the
fabric of our bold, tender nature
they appear like home around
the table

When we gather together
we remember who we are
as we sip our earl grey
with the familiar tap of
mugs on wood and scent
of bergamot uniting the
space between us

We are home.

for Christmas I
bought myself purple
lipstick
and said
"I will wear this
every day
until I am no
longer afraid"

—*transition*

a love letter to my body:

every time I take a
bath, I kiss my kneecaps
and massage between
my toes

I let the water hold me how I
long to be held
and the salt of the earth
eases away the ache

underwater, I listen to
my heart beat
lighting seven tiny
candles, I ask for what
I need, what I
want

and open my heart

I feel afraid
every day
it is a feeling
I have spent
years trying to be
friends with

sometimes we
sit next to each other
and soak in the sun

this feels like something
this feels like healing

I forgot how to pray
with the structured words
of my teachers
and preachers

and remembered how to dance
with the colors and moans
and songs of my ancestors

I light a candle to open the way
clear out the static and begin to
manifest
I dance around with cinnamon
and rosemary and make
magic in the kitchen
I listen with my mind relaxed like
a kitten in the sun
while the plants grow and breathe
out oxygen

to be present to this moment and not
want to skip ahead
to bloom when I bloom
to decay when I decay
to love with a heart full of roses
and a soul rooted with the slow grace
of trees, quiet and old
growing together with ferns at our feet

let me make magic
I say

let me dance every day for as long as
I can still move my body
let me know the tenderness of embraces
in all their supple forms and welcome
the touch of love and hope
upon my shoulders like
hugging my best friend

let me be here now
and not want to just move on
welcoming the sun, rising in pink and orange
glory over the fields
where the hummingbirds
play and the songs of the wind
and the leaves humm and murmur

I am here
I am here
I am here

there are sleeping
butterflies growing in the
curving bones
of my rib cage

they unfurl their
wings when I forget
to dream, and awaken
when I open myself
to the light

when I'm old, maybe
my back will be a
record of their flight
with wings like scars
opening and
disappearing into
my shoulder blades
like we are
made for each other

tears have been a character in the
story of my life since my first
joyful *yes I am here in this world*
scream through sobs alone, my arms
wrapped about me, to tears
streaming down my face freely, with
friends laughing until we cry.

hello
hello
hello

I looked at my face tonight
in the mirror, and for the
first time said,
"wow, you are really
pretty" and smiled
back at myself, while I
soaked in my own love

there's a difference between
not hating yourself and
loving yourself
between saying, "you're not
awful" to "you are
lovely"

it's like flowers bursting
into bloom in great gulps
of color and joy
while the sun caresses
the earth with her warmth

how I long to be warm

I want to know the
names of trees
and cry when
they die

I will write my
life as a poem

because poetry is
the only language
I know without
thinking

it is the way I
breathe, the way
I drink my tea
the way I watch
the sun rise and
sparkle in the
morning

sometimes my feelings
run out my eyes
big teary gulps
and quiet lonely
raindrops

joy, grief, happiness
confusion—somehow
form and shift into
water, cascading over
the ache in my chest

gathering like friends
and lovers on my cheeks
hanging on for
one last moment before
slipping off my eyelashes
streaking rivers
through the terrain of
a face of many smiles

how many lessons the water has
to whisper into my collarbone
and wash my heart with
salt and surrender

and in this moment
I want to be
willing

today I asked
the pain throbbing
in my temples
and pulsing through
my head

"what do you want?"

to be heard

"I hear you," I
whispered, "I hear
you"

*I think of you
in the silence between
moments
while I'm waiting for
sleep to come
when my mind
wanders to the land of
dreams and my heart
relaxes for a moment*

this morning I awoke
to the sound of laughter in the kitchen
and dear friends sharing their
dreams

to a kitten curled by
my feet
and the fog tickling
the trees

how happy I am
to be alive

what is it to witness a soul?
to remain still and calm
and quiet enough
for the shy
truth of being to
emerge, explore
wander, shine

it happens, sometimes
in the dark of night
when one person's body
is sick beyond
exhaustion, and another
kind soul waits in
quiet comfort, through
hours of torment
making tea, and speaking
with words sparsely sprinkled
until morning comes
with the hope of rest

to witness happens
at the edge of the
ocean, where the roar
of power and ever turning
tides coax the shy
wounded being out in
a song, or bought of
tears, while the waters

hold space for an
eternal moment

I have been seen
most clearly in joy and
sorrow when another
is present beside me
like a quiet forest
open to the tender
wildness of my living

may we see one another
may we see ourselves

imagine how we could
love each other now
after all these years

what beautifully complex
people we have become

how I want to
return to your safe
embrace, to trace the
freckles on your back
and let our kisses
rest their way
back together

if love is like an
ocean, then you are
the stars, singing her
to life, night after night

I remember the water
dark and full of mystery
my dad offering a quarter
to the first kid to jump
my heart pounding
my feet leaving the creaky
wooden dock
the water, sliding and then
crashing into my body, my
mouth, my nose, my lungs

I remember my feet
pushing against the deep
and my eyes finding light
and my lungs, never so
happy to breathe again

I remember sitting
with a towel on my shoulders
turning over quarter
again and again between my
fingertips, watching
while everyone else
played and laughed
and swam

I did not go back in.

my heart expands
like a wildfire
crashing through the
woods, scaring the
birds into flight
and the forest creatures
away from their
homes

my heart loves
like a whirlwind
upsetting everything
still and quiet and
breathing life in such
great gusts as to
never leave
room for life
without

my heart aches like
an avalanche, loud
and sudden, pouring
tears over rocks
stirring up dust like
ashes resting on
shoulders tumbling
down

my heart is a
powerful thing, a life-force
beyond reckoning
I feel with the wideness
of the earth
the desperation of every
rain soaked day
the hope of every
river running to the sea

who am I to
argue with fire?

I love the corner of
your lips when you
smile
I love the look you
get, when everything
outside this moment
disappears

for that smile
for those eyes
I wish I could
give you the stars
and kiss every
dimpled cheek
and sparkle back
the sun

and oh how I would adore you

who am I
without defenses?

what would you
see of me, with
the curtains pulled
back, and the walls
left unbuilt?

would you see
me then, and
would I be what
you expected?

acceptance smells like
spiced vanilla on my
fingertips, and rings
like the notes of your
voice when you
think no one
is listening

I hear you
I know you
I see you

and everything
about this moment
is magic, where
happiness kisses
the earth like the stars
kiss the sky
like my breath
finds yours
and there's no need
to talk anymore

and I'm here

earl grey
is a balm
to my soul

when I sip this
strong and tender
liquid, I am
transported to a
knowing

that I am here
now, and here is a
place I can breathe

when I die
I want to become
a field of flowers

and every winter
when I lose my leaves
and the last flower falls

I will turn into stars

and be born again
into flowers
every spring

"can I read you a poem
I wrote today?" is a
question often found on
my lips, on the edge
of sound as my mouth
naturally asks the
question

people think it's brave
to share my work like this
so ordinarily, so casually

and maybe it is

all I know is that my
heart explodes with her
own silence when I keep
it in, and words written
in my notebook sometimes
beg and sing to be
shared

I want to be playful
to jump with abandon into
the magic of this moment
soaked in sorrow and aching
in the in-between places of
my spine

I want to ride on wings
and where will I go?
Where are the sparks on
the wind? do I see
them, or feel them,
or wander into them at
the last moments
when my breath is
almost gone and I
am finally here?

do I love my tea in the
morning
because it is made of
you and me?
water—seen, collected
alive
bergamot—sensuous, earthy
unfolding
black tea—potent, energizing
gathering

when I drink this
I feel our collective love
our generational remembering
the groundness in our flow
the openness of who we are

my life is a poem
I write a few new lines
every morning

I guess you could say
I'm praying
sitting on a log in the
woods, surrounded by
poison oak
watching spider webs
shimmer and shift
in the breeze while
the sun gazes on
us all

dogs pass by with
their humans
curious and happy
to be so *in* the dirt
I hear many conversations
and slow whispers from
the trees

a sprout pushes up
through decaying leaves
near my boot on the ground
I drink water
and give thanks

writing is like that
breath I must take
coming up to the surface
after swimming underwater

sometimes I arrive
choking, struggling
flapping my arms like wings

sometimes gracefully
my feet finding kinship
with their mermaid cousins

all I know
is that I must breathe

I want to weave
my voice with yours
with your hands
in my hair
and your breath
on my collarbone

oh the music
we could make

in the center of the
stillness, when I am quiet
enough to sink deep into myself
past the noise and
worries and wonderings
the things I feel anxious
about and everything I want

I find a circle
of all my favorite people
sitting around a fire

I sigh as I feel their
welcome, their beckoning
to come and be.
my grandma hands
me a cup of hot cocoa
winks at me, and smiles
the dawn, where light
comes back in
to darkness

slowly, I let myself
let go
pushing everything from
outside this moment past
my clenched fingers
as fear drifts away
from my aching chest

how warm it is
to be here, now with
love around me
to know only this
moment, and these
faces, and the light
warming my toes
and my heart
letting me breathe again

how lovely to find that
I don't have to have
everything in order
to rest, everything done
to be here, now

my body opens to you
like a flower
kissed with sunlight
your fingertips find me
like they've been searching
for home

and are you
trying to kiss every
part of me?

to kiss away all
the ache
with no hurry
no expectation

and how you soak into
me like the warmth
of the sun setting
spreading over
the curves and
valleys of my body, and
answering every question
with your arms
around me
and eyes that
speak fire

my heart feels
heavy today
with rocks like all the words
I want to say
sprawled and scattered
in the ocean of my
chest
sinking and falling and
floating
they make melodies with
their aching
and I'm just waiting to burst
open and become
undone

rivers flow from my
aching body
like blood turning
water red
like the way my
feelings drown out my
eyes and ring like
bells in an echo
chamber losing
sight and sound
and grounding
as all I see and
hear are notes
that blend and
bleed, breaking me
slowly from the
inside

is this then, how I pray?

forgetting you is harder
than I thought
mostly because
I don't want to

letting you go
and watching the
possibilities of
us tangled up
together drift
away
like they were
never there

it's hard to let
go of some exciting
things that was
almost
some beautiful idea
not fully formed
a breath half-breathed and
forgotten

but what am I to do?
weave you into the
skies of my existence?
tattoo you in the stars
of my questions
and wanderings
and love?

stars become stars

when we can't carry
them
anymore

the ground has changed
so much and so have I
these feet have wandered
and shook and danced
they have laughed in my
toes and cried in my
heels

forest floor, with your
roots and ferns and soil
alive in every speck,
will you help me heal?
will you help me be here
now, even as I will move
and wander and dance
and shake, again?

*looking at the
stars in the trees
tonight*

I dream of you

I want to be lost
in you for a moment
but I'm afraid

afraid of softness
afraid of the fragility
that blankets me
like your arms
circling my body
warm and caring
safe and soft

my lips know a language
my words will never understand

there is magic in their softness

stepping into the
stream of my unconscious
washing over me
like waterfall waves
pulsing against the
blood beneath my skin

am I magic?
or mystery?

am I found here
lost in myself
relaxing my mind
like a drug, accepting
the wild unknowing
of how my
heart continues
to beat day after day
and how I am
not yet undone?

pain is a familiar skin
I dress in every morning
and wrap myself
in like sheets in the night

if someone told me
"you could have a new
skin" or I thought
to myself *I could sleep
naked*

how unfamiliar it would
feel to wrap myself in—
what is the absence of
pain?

love?

softness?

delight?

I want to laugh
every day of my
life

and when I
die, I will
become
joy

grass grows
again and again
in the same spot

what else
is the definition
of tenacity?

a year ago, I received
visions of the future—
of how I would meet
my fears, one after the
other, in all their
terrifying glory

how I would meet them
and see them
and not run away

how I would feel all
the terror again, how I
would revisit my
darkest corners
and not be overcome

and here I am

my heart is beating
out of my chest like a
drum so loud all I
can do is listen
and be caught up
in the sound
while it echoes and
moves me like
music, asking me
to open my hands
clenched tightly
and beckoning me
to find freedom
in just listening
in just being
in the drum
in the steady, powerful
declaration
I'm alive
I'm here
pay attention

when I feel sad
I wear earrings my
grandmother gave
me as a child

little amethyst studs
that speak as rocks
do—

this too will
pass, and I
I will still be here

some things we bought
together are slowly
becoming nothing

in the rain and the sun
giving up their substance
letting go

and others

house tomato starts
and spicy peppers
are the caravans
for meals and
cereal in the morning

it is all of this
all mixed together

a query to my heart:

what do you think about
while you beat inside my
chest, filling my body with
the moment of life?

someone made a painting
that said, "the universe
loves you"

when I read these words
my heart jumped with
a little "oh"

and I was surprised
by tears swelling and
swimming in my eyes

is this what it feels
like, to find the language
of home?

we started this
thing with crying
in the park
and since have
too many moments
to collect with words

I am better for
your pink-purple hair
for the shit you talk
about boys who need it
by your angsty glory
by our moments
in the kitchen
and finding truths
in tarot cards and the
laughter of our stars

With your hands you
wove a fabric masterpiece
with your lies and
half-truths and
subtle pushes and hushes
and "no actually, it's
not like that" that I'm
choking on the cloth
woven inside me
gagging on moments put
in boxes labeled do-not-
open, or remember
or believe

it may take me time
but I will unwind you
from my flesh
untie you from my bones
unwrite you from my heart

I call bullshit on your lies

I want to eject you
from my body
my eyes want to throw you up
my ears want to spit you out
my hands bleed rivers
and my stomach
swirls and heaves

what did you do to me?

"what did he do to you?"
you whispered, agonized
trying to hold my
shaking body close
while I pushed you back

it wasn't just him
my bones scream
and my skin shivers

I couldn't take you anymore
but I wasn't brave
enough yet to let
the words out

I waited, while our "we"
slowly died
I am strong despite you

I'm redefining love
from any way I've known it
with all its monsters
in the cabinets
and shadows under
the bed

my, what a wild
beautiful creature
you are

your tree hands are cold
and guarded, slowly thawing
with the warmth of our
fingers and palms holding
space like ice, then fire

will you let me in?
let me see you and whisper
warmth into your tightly
guarded home of a
body?

we can create
stars with our magic and
watch sparks on the
wind, finding all the
ways to come alive and let
go, finding freedom
as we rise

I always thought
softness was weakness
that by letting my
body relax
or gentleness live
on my fingertips
that I was somehow
letting go
somehow sacrificing
my bravery

now I see, to be soft
is majestically courageous

I can see us there
you sitting in the sun-
drenched doorway
me kissing the top of your head
us laying in fields of
tiny white flowers, my
red curls mixing with your
long dark waves

how I long to intertwine
my fingers in yours
to kiss you and know
the time is right
to hold you softly
to love you openly

I often finish my dad's
sentences, reading his
thoughts easily because
we have the same
tides flowing through us
the same knowings
the same curious expression

wondering at the world

I learned opening from my mother
how to open the day with
ritual and quiet
how to open dreams like flowers
how to open my heart to love

I learned closing from my father
how to close the day with reflection
and ritual
how to take a breath and savor the
moments before something ends
how to cry in all the sad movies

between the rosebuds
and the thorns
the pine tree branches
with their needles
and kitty claws

my hands are
always bleeding

and turning up
scars that cry, "I'm alive,
I feel it. I feel it all"
and then falling
back into whispers
while my body
heals itself
one more time

to the giants who
live in the mountains
under the trees:

I see you
I want to hear
your story
to know your
voice as old as
beginning

thank you for
watching over us

I wanted every door
left open, while I
danced in the kitchen
in the darkest dark
of the night

I wanted to feel
that everyone was
still breathing, still
here, not gone yet

I was existing in a
time here, not yet,
and everywhere at once

I needed to know
I wasn't alone

for Christmas I gave
everyone in my family
a white tea light

to remember the time
they held me while I
was shaking and singing
and maybe dying

to honor the vigil of
space they created while
I traveled the universe
and came back to myself

to laugh at how many
candles I lit, and how they
hid the matches

pain is a lesson
I am always
learning

it's like my heart hands mouth
body is reaching for something
with so much wanting
that my own need
might explode my heart

—desire

am I a lover?
or a revolutionary?

does the way I bring
myself to the world—
heart open
arms ready to hold
noticing every flower
along the way—

change the world?
to be a tiny bit
more open,
a tiny bit
more whole?

when I'm suffering
I harvest the fruits
of my resilience

I collect the sweet honey
blossoms of my
softness

I lay back in the
storehouse of my
ability to rest

sometimes I want
all the pain
to leave my body

sometimes it
does, and I don't
remember how to
feel this calm

—awakening

red, like the blood
collecting in the base
of my body
as the full moon
crowns in the sky
and my belly
squeezes and cries
shedding dreams
and aches
and echoes and
hallelujahs

the difference between pain
and surrender
is how long before I cry
before tears of
water and salt and
blood leave my body
like a snake shedding
her skin, aching
and alone in the
night, to be
reborn in the morning

when I die
I want to become
a jellyfish

and live forever
in the arms of
the sea

when the sun peeks over the horizon to greet
the day and spread golden honey warmth
to the dark, sleepy earth

when the birds begin to stir and twitter
and tune their songs to one another

when the trees rustle as the morning breeze
opens her eyes from slumber, and the dew is heavy
on the blades of grass

when I know morning has come once again
and we are not lost to the night, even as we
are not lost to the day

light dawns, and I can move again
breathing in streams of fresh morning air
lighting a candle for rejuvenation
and praying the day in with ginger and
salt and clay

oh how lovely it feels to be alive
how magical to wake with the light
and live

*I want to kiss you
until you are
undone
until your breath
collapses with pleasure
and your body
surrenders all thought
and questions
and you are
free*

how lucky I am
to wake up next
to you
with my hand
on your hip
and my lips
against your
shoulder blade

if courage is being
afraid all the time
and still living

I am one of the
bravest people
I know

from you I learned simplicity
the ability to be
in a moment
and wonder.

some words need to be
repeated
the way a sunset plays
every night in the
fade to twilight
the same scene
over and over
but never once
lost
in its sameness

my heart spoke. my feet listened.

I have fields of flowers
named after you
after your hands
after the sparkle playing
in your eyes when you smile
after the moments
you let all your armor down
and I see you in all your
complexity and softness

in case there was any doubt

if I were a season
I would be
spring.

signs I might be a fairy:

*finding moss on my
clothes*

*feeling relief when my
fingers touch a tree*

*ferns are the most
beautiful thing I can imagine*

you call me
springtime
and whisper that
I am made of stars

you believe in my
soft, striking magic
more than I hoped
another person could

how you fill my
skies with flowers

the bubbles in my stomach feel like
echoes of how grounded I long to be but
somehow can't land

there's too much water mixed with
anxious, half-formed thoughts and over
thought thoughts and fears that I'll be
floating and wandering around here
forever

my potted plant heart is overflowing with water
drowning out my roots and stripping my soil
of what I need

how do I wade through all of these
feelings? is there a way forward where I can
face myself and not feel
afraid?

you may see the
softness of my smile
the lightness of my voice
the bubbling water of my
laughter

but do you also know
the steel in my bones
the fire in my eyes
the power in my hands?

and there were all the hallelujahs
and there were all the hallelujahs
and there were all the hallelujahs

I am connected to
every person I have
ever loved, in any way

I feel their heart
beats when I listen
with my heart
expanded like a
universe of stars

their sighs are the
wind in my trees
their tears, the
rain on my window

the ground has changed
so much and so have I
these feet have wandered
and shook and danced
they have laughed in my
toes and cried in
my heels

forest floor, with your
roots and ferns and soil
alive in every speck—
will you help me heal?
will you help me be here
now, even as I will move
and wander and dance
and shake again?

let me be the place in your heart
where joy lives

let us make miracles with
our laughter
and magic with our fingers
intertwined

let's wander the woods
like fairies, stopping to
feel the moss on our
toes and listen to the
heartbeats of trees

let us breathe fire into the
cold, dark places you hold so tightly
and watch the light
grow and glow

let us create a space
where warmth and sorrow
can co-exist, where you
can be all of you
and relax into the
silence

let me be the place in your heart
where joy lives

to be such an
embodied being
in such a
sensitive body

sometimes feels like dying
like carrying all
the pain around me in
the crook of my neck
and the sorrow of those
I hold in the heavy
aching, I-can-almost-bear-it-
no-longer muscles
crawling up my spine

to my right temple:

how much of my life you
spend throbbing

it is a miracle you are still going

what are you fighting?
why don't you let go?

my body overflows with
water. am I drowning from
the inside?

I want to be
washed clean, to find
resolution in the
waves pouring over
my heart-aching body
opening me to the
wild beauty of
feelings honestly felt and
breathing, seeing myself
in the mirror of
the river, flowing
over the dynamic
shifts and dips and
rhythms of my
being

I want to find how to
live with you and not
against you
to rise from the ocean
anew from my journey
through the fire
to the openness and
power of the sea
freed from the closeness of
my fear, swimming
with angels and demons
alike

as I rise
as I rise
as I rise

my life is about to change
forever, shifting just
enough for a dramatic
entrance and deep dive into
welcoming waters of
unknown

I can still breathe here

to be the wings of a
butterfly and feel
the air tickle and
flow about me as
I fly

I want to be so
light, so full of
light that I soar

to stretch out my
arms and fall
through the clouds
feeling the magic
of life in breath
everywhere

to be so unafraid to
float, to surrender to the
wind

and where will you
carry me, take me?
how will it feel to
let everything go?

I take love advice from
poem after poem by
my most sacred poets
one poem can change

everything

the way the light
holds your face
and your tiny hands
grasp a flower
like it may be the
last beautiful thing
you know how
to believe in

—*sadness {inspired by Common Ground,
a photography series with portraits of
Afghan refugees}*

a year ago I chose the
path of the wanderer
the dream traveler
the shapeshifter

the magician
the mystic
the star child

I want to give myself
to the wind
bringing healing like
a cup of cool water
everywhere I go

I am made of stars

a bowl full of butterflies

*are they still?
do they move when I blink?*

*are they actually alive in their
painted colors, glittering
gold on edges of tiny wings?*

do they breathe?

when you've seen
too much
too soon

and loss becomes
more than the feeling
that tears everything
out of your chest
and turns into
the air coming
unbidden into your
lungs

—*refugee {inspired by Common Ground,
a photography series with portraits of
Afghan refugees}*

I wear bright colors
so I can see myself

I wear bright colors
because joy is my middle finger

I wear bright colors
because I will not be afraid

*talking to you
feels like coming home*

*our friendship is like
a deep sigh at the edge
of dusk in summer*

*our hearts rest
while we watch the
stars come alive*

I am a sojourner
in winter

I wander the empty
landscapes of rainy sky
and lonely places of my heart with
uncertain intention and
delicate hope

but when spring comes

I am home.

I don't know what is more
shattering

to see your eyes
sparkle and break

or the back of your
head, the way sorrow has
shaped your shoulders into
mountains

*{inspired by Common Ground,
a photography series with portraits of
Afghan refugees}*

I often sit under the
red oak whose trunk lives
over the fence and
whose roots live beneath my feet
her canopy towers above me
bright and green with
the songs of wind and
magic in the springtime

*how lovely you are
to share your glory*

the sky wakes so early
the soft blue-grey of the morning
gentle against the harsh
shadows of trees still sleeping
their branches etched
in the moments between
darkness and the warm glow
of a sun on the way

*I feel you on my skin
mixed with dirt from the garden
and the warm kiss of sunshine*

*how I love to be
held by you
and even
the warmth that lingers
next to the freckles
on my shoulders
and under my cheekbones*

after you go

when I see you
I see a leaf

not the hundred
tiny veins that run
red and green
through your body

exhaling life

I must have been
a bird in some past life

when I spread my
wings in dreams

I am never afraid

happiness is
the feeling of your arms
around me and the
way they whisper
"I will never get
tired of
holding you"

sometimes my hands
have a knowing
beyond my busy mind

the day before spring came
I was overcome by the flowers
I see through my window

with my ritual of ushering
I filled a jar with water
asked with my fingers who
wanted to come inside
and put them happily
at the center of the table

what a welcome
my hands have learned

once, I drew a bath
for pain
I carried her battered
body and let
the hot healing water cradle her

I put flowers around
her and called in fireflies
who landed like lights
among the petals

while I watched
she began to die
and at the last moment
her body became
one thousand bright
blue butterflies

I will never be the same

*let me be in this
moment*

*with the lacy evening
foam tracing the
orange sun kissed
sand*

*let the waves take
my heart and
bring me home*

letter to my 14-year-old
high school self:

it's ok to like girls

*your body is made of
magic, and nothing to be
afraid of*

*do not fear, brave little fashionista
you'll find your way*

I never knew there were
so many rocks in my body
until I asked sadness,
where do you live?

and then I saw the rocks
hanging like wind chimes
around my throat
and felt them buried
around the mountainous
terrain of my shoulder blades

when I saw pain
her twisted mangled
aching not quite there
form of a body

I surprised myself

and kissed her fingertips
I kissed her hands
until they were hands
I kissed her until
she had form and
skin and matter and a body

while I wept a sky
full of tears

there's a fire in every
room of my heart today
and in my belly, too

candles flicker, with their
waxy resistance to air
and water and earth
as somehow the
flame continues to
ignite

and I am bathed in their
light, in my light, in the
light created with the
people I love and those
who gave me these candles I
didn't yet know I needed

how many places can
be alight before I
accept that I am not alone?

even in the darkness
there are stars in my
palms and the soles of my feet
and buried deep in the
soil of my heart

and for this moment
I am warm
and warmed by the
lights carrying me home

there are many plants
in my bedroom
shifting their leafy
bodies constantly and slowly
toward the sun

some days I awake
and find them taller
with a leaf freshly
born and created
in the night, peering
out into the brand
new dawn

oh, to be so present
to the day
so willing in the night
so faithful to create

yesterday I hung on to a tree at the top of
a mountain, while the wind shook the sky and the trees
and me

as I held closely to this tree that I deeply hoped was
more rooted than I and felt the great gusts
sweeping past me and through me

did I have time to be afraid?

I felt my whole body tense with the possibility of
being thrown overboard by the wind, I felt fear well up
in my chest and my fingertips holding on to my
new tree-best-friend for dear life and coursing
through my feet that felt not solid enough
not here enough

I spoke to the wind: "take away my fear"
and with the next gail, holding on with my
body, I let go with my heart
and watched pieces of me fly over the
valley and land among the trees
and jump and swim in the waters

to be alive with my fear, to stand in the
wind held by trees, how wondrous that
my lungs continue to fill with
air, how stunning that those trees
stay rooted at the very top

how alive I am today

we wash and perfume
our bodies like we wash
and perfume the dead
bodies of those we
love and those we
tolerate

being alive
is an active
creation
and death is
a slow
surrender

I give myself
every smile ready to brighten
every hug waiting in my arms
every kiss on the forehead
every foot massage
every whispered *you are not alone*
every quiet sigh of relief
every offering of my hands to heal

I want to be a
waterfall of love

I want to be this for me

I'm afraid for the
love that is ready

for the one who says yes
who looks back at me
and we know
the time is right

what will it be like
to live with such clarity?

for all those dark days
when I couldn't see myself
when I couldn't get up
from the wooden floor boards
when to be touched felt
like I would never be ok again

to the me that survived:

I still see you
I won't forget you
you're not trapped anymore

are my headaches aftershocks
of believing that I didn't have
a voice?

does my head throb and
scream for all the times
I was silent and all the
ways I was taught
to give myself away?

will they stop when I
speak again? when I
sing? shout?
hear myself?

there's a pocket in my stomach
where anxiety still lives

she isn't a roaring
fire, burning me quickly
out of control, take-over-
my-body
presence, anymore

now she is a
candle in a jar
who explodes
from time to time

untangling myself
from the religion of my childhood

is like discovering
I was tied down to a
sunken ship
existing at the ocean's floor

I didn't know I could swim
I didn't know the sun existed
I didn't know my body is my own
I didn't know how to breathe

I know that innocence
is a temporary stage
that forming a protective
shell is a part of becoming

what rough teachers I have

I have had a headache
for seven years

one day
I will wake up
and it will be gone

until then

I am learning
how to breathe

when I was 19, my
greatest fear was that
I would have a sad story

I wept over plays and stories
of love lost, of love not
fulfilled, not realized

perhaps I thought that
sadness is a force greater
than love
that love is only everything
if it is held forever

but love is air
any breath I take
any moment of compassion
any time my body holds yours
any time and space
shared and held
between us

*we can breathe out love
along with sadness*

do you know
that I am free
without you?

to be broken
is not to be lost
I have been shattered
many times
and risen again

resurrection
is not an old story from a book

it is this:
my body learning to feel calm
my bare feet sinking into soil
the ways I am becoming

I was baptized
under snow
in hot water
a celebration and
the beginning of my 9th
year of life

I don't remember the words
but I remember the water
and the feeling of snow
meeting my eyelashes
when I rose

I was born in water
and born again
how my body remembers
this truth like a sigh
how the water welcomes me
each time and whispers:

you can be free now
you can rise

in the morning, I water the garden
and steep my tea
I drape a blanket over
my rocking chair
and watch tomatoes and
spicy peppers flower and
form, grape leaves
shimmer as they uncurl
and prance over the grass

my kitty companion lays on my toes
I am glad to be in this
breath, in this space
where I can rest lightly
on the earth, alive in
this moment

my mother can talk
to cats.
they come to her and whisper
their names

she listens without hesitation

—lessons

there are bees in my body
I am abuzz with electricity

I do not need more

but oh how they
swarm and buzz and sting
congregating in my temples

I am on fire with them

my laughter is its own
language

I can say
I love you
you're ridiculous
don't ever stop being the
way you are

or wait, stay
with me, in this moment

without ever pulling
words from my tongue

the stars in my eyes
the ocean in yours

together

we see the universe

sometimes I feel like I am
hiding in my body

how can so many
stars and waves and
leaves

inhabit this little set of
eyes and arms
and toes?

there is the truth that
lives in the chaotic
cauldron of my heart

bubbling and uncertain
overflowing every moment
orange and red

and then there is
the truth that leaves
my throat
in streams of blue
flying from the container
of my body

to the place in my spine
I can't feel:

you became so full of
agony that you disappeared

or I disappeared from you

you contain multitudes
chaotic lessons of resilience
and compassion
of paying attention
and letting go

will you share your lessons?
will you let the snake of
my spine swallow you
and give yourself to
my body?

I pray more now
than I ever have
and prayer is no longer
something I do with
my eyes closed
or my head down

I am alive in the
sensation of it
the flick of the match
the sizzle of the flame to
wick, the whisper
of the goddess

sometimes my body
feels like a leaf

and the winds of
the world
pass through me

I want to settle into the
rocky bottom, sinking between
the bright smooth stones

under the seas of my life

I remember our
last night together
how we held each other
fiercely and tenderly

how our arms
never left one another's
bodies

how we woke
in the morning
to say goodbye

I don't tell you how
bad it was

because I'm afraid
you'll never look at me
the same

why do I assume
you won't see the
strength I have
flooding my veins
burning my bones
driving my heart

to have survived?

I didn't know
that believing in magic
would help me believe
in hope again

I didn't know that
my greatest teachers
would be cats and
plants and spiders
pots of soup and
turmeric potions

that by believing in
magic, I could be
two hands and a heart
open in the swell
of healing
the creation of life

my belly is a treasure
cave of strange mementos

sparky anxiety here
decomposing memories there
pearls created from
irritation
artifacts from lovers
echoes of panic attacks
crayon paintings of my
childhood fears

and also

hope
knowing what it is to be alive
power in who I am becoming

*I discovered by accident
that my throat has
wings*

*not the delicate petals
of a butterfly
but the strong sweeping
weather-y wings
of a dragon*

*and I thought
all this time my voice was
trapped
that you were a cage
I couldn't exist without*

*but now
I can fly*

*I love the way leaves
turn toward the sun
while they are growing*

*they want so openly
there is no shame
in their desire*

*so they sigh
and bathe in light*

wanting has left a
chasm in my chest

when I first discovered
the desperate vastness
and untamable sadness

I ran away

but I have returned
each day, with a bouquet
of flowers, to sit
with my grief, to feel the
ache of longing left
unfulfilled

this too

a year ago I wondered
if I was making the right choice

if the leaving
the complicated messy
untangling
was right

when my heart was aching
and my body crying
and panicked

yes

I want to whisper to her now

yes

it gets better soon

you looked at me
with eyes that know
the future
in the stretchy magic
of time
and said:

when you are done
you will be a superhero

you will fly

I let myself out in
pieces

afraid
that if I am all of me
at once

I will break the world
or even
you will see me and turn
away

*I could fall for you
as easy as closing
my eyes when you
say my name*

*my eyelashes
nestling in with one
another*

*seeing the surprise
and delight in your
eyes when I pull
you close*

*the way your hands
cradle my body*

I am dramatic
I love quickly
my heart is a powerful
thing in my body

and timing is a bitch

when I was 8 years old
I was buried by snow
rushing from the roof, chasing
my tiny body

that is when I learned
what it feels like to be trapped
what panic is
how the body shakes when
it can't breathe

I don't remember anything
after the moment I
saw light again and my
screaming stopped
my parents faces through the snow
and hands pulling me up

letter to my jaw:

what are you afraid of?
thank you for being
a gate of discernment
for letting out what
you know to be true

don't hold back
you do not need to be
everything
you can let go

my room feels messy
with you
tousled with your
laughter, sprinkled with
the sparks in your
eyes when you smile

how do you make me
more at home?

what does it mean to
not be alone?

does it mean laying in
the sand, eyes closed
body heavy with
rocks, sun soaking in
asking each part of my
body, "what do you need?"
and when I get to my throat

suddenly
there is a
family of femmes carrying
baskets across my shoulders
each taking a stone
and laboring it away
with the power of their bodies

they found rocks I didn't know existed
I don't know how to feel this light

to my muscles, strong and
tense throughout my body:

thank you for protecting me
thank you for knowing when
something isn't right
thank you for the way
you hold my bones and
let me move

you can breathe now
I am listening

my family is
water, water, water

the people who held me
made me
adventured with me
poured their love into me

and I am earth
oh what a vessel
what a glorious, surprising
plant filled vessel

I was raised in a house of water

I am learning to feel the
back of my heart
the place where it
beats life against
my spine
the place where it
can rest against
my ribcage

how cold you feel
how I hope you can trust
the strength in my bones

a letter to my ribcage:

do you remember being
crushed? the feeling of
air jolting out of your body
the dark blank
am-I-really-here
is-this-really-happening
-ness of the moment?

how you wanted your
grandmother's arms to
hold your little body
and whisper that
it won't last forever

and how you were told instead
it's not that bad
and made to wait
for hours before
comfort could arrive

is this when you learned
that trusting is dangerous?

to watch my father grow older
is to see a tired, beaten man
soften
and bloom

discover joy, despite
and within
and around
pain

to see him dance
and giggle
to see his eyes
sparkle with some new
truth he's discovered

you have your own
medicine in your body

they tell me while their
hands seek out places
that ache

you have what you need
you have what you need
you have what you need

it took me a year to be angry
and maybe a lifetime to understand
why

you hurt me with your words
the way I felt like I
couldn't say no

the way our lives were
so tangled up together
that I felt lost within us

and you blamed me
for losing yourself
for taking up space
for being full of light

even as you sucked the
life from my bones

I won't tell anyone
you whispered
with your slimy hands
discovering my body

and to each *no, no, no*
you responded with
more more more

I threw away the
clothes I wore that night

what is it about "no"
that you see as an invitation,
a negotiation?

don't you bastards
understand that
just because you
want something

doesn't mean you will get it

you can listen

you blamed me
for being difficult
for not doing enough
trying enough
being enough

don't you see how
that destroyed me?

when you saw me in my
new life, you cried
and said you missed me

are you jealous that I am
happy without you?

Anger and love can
co-exist
and that's what makes
the leaving

ache

because it's all tangled
up together
because of all the things
I couldn't see until I was gone
because I would have been
lost forever if I stayed

I am sick with you
my body wants to throw you up
expel you from my memory

empty you from my mind
remove you from my heart

my own ability to not
see reality when it's crashing into my body
continues to surprise me

how did I not know?
how could I not see?

you were hurting me
and I called it love

your heart may catch fire
the cards say
don't be afraid of the darkness

something new is happening
something wonderful
like clouds floating on the
blue ocean of the sky
like sea creatures
embracing the ripples
of waves above

open your heart

I was born in water
born again
and again

buried in water
drowned in water
found in water

I feel my heart breaking
and I don't even know how
I opened to you so quickly

when you walked back into
my life in a dream
and then the moment I saw your
face, heard your voice,
felt your strong hands
hold my body

warmth flooded my chest
and I thought it was fate
I thought, say the word
this is it

I don't want to imagine
a world where we don't
love each other

and yet
I might break in the waiting

I'm afraid you'll think
I'm dramatic, or too much
too soon

I'm afraid you'll judge my
love, my affection, my openness

I'm afraid that it will scare you
and you'll walk away
because you're not ready
or you don't want me

how much can I
open to you
pour affection and
tenderness in
give you an open
invitation to my
bed, my heart, my life

and wait until you're
ready?

what if you are never
ready?

full moon notes:

drink water
let go
be renewed

you are stars and
earth, fire and rain

you are full of love

to the fear buried in
my stomach:

thank you

for helping me see danger
for sending messages
to navigate this wild
explosive world

you can speak quieter now
I will listen

if you don't love me
tell me
so I can break already

waiting
is agony

hope is the most
dangerous weapon
I use against myself

like the dream of your
arms around me
like closing my eyes
and seeing
you, you, you

can I survive this
uncertainty?

when I get angry
I massage my hands
I whisper into my fingertips

I love you
I love you
I love you
I love you
I love you
I love you

because I was taught to be
angry is to be a monster
and I don't want to
hate any part of me

anymore

wanting you is like
wanting an explosion

at any moment my
fingertips will catch fire
and my heart will
beat shock waves through
my body

I cannot contain this
much desire
and not be

fireworks

*there are horses
in your voice
running along the
cage of your throat*

let them free

this morning I watched
tiny yellow finches
pluck wishes off
dandelions

what do you wish for,
little birds?

is it a song?

you love me you love me
you love me you love me
you love me you love me

that is my wish, too

all of my poems
are about me

and you

they are about
being in
relation

about the threads
we weave
the world

I'm sitting here writing
dramatic poetry that I
will probably never read
to you

because *(for now)* I am ashamed
at how much my heart
wants, and how freely
she demands it

today I filled my
bones with love

and then snuggled up
in the knowledge

that every move
of my body
can come from love

a raven walked
across the rooftop
one foot in front of
the other

how simple
how ordinary
how extravagant

*but you know
it's going to hurt
if you live with your
heart wide open*

*they say, with their
worried faces and
crumpled up eyebrows*

yes

*I say, with whispers of grief
deeper than the ocean
singing at the bottom of
my lungs*

yes

but my heart is a fire

I write of the delicate
landscapes of the heart
the dramatic flowers
from the sky
body shaking
moments along the
way of healing
and offer them to the world

and yet

there are some poems
I read only to myself

my room smells of
roses, plants grow toward
the sun

I sit under a shower of
curtains, my heart reaching
arms around my body

holding myself
in beauty
while my body shakes
with pain

under me, a fabric sea
of stars

I tell stories with my poetry
I write my memories in
stars and ink
my meditations in
rose petals and propositions
the tensions and truth
of my life in
jagged lines and metaphor

I cannot hold all this
inside me

I made you a daisy crown
and you laughed
and smiled with your eyes

"I'm honored"
you said
while I slid
white daisies into your
long dark hair

—new

I told you in the kitchen
how I walked a
labyrinth alone at sunset
and in the center petals
I played my harmonica
to the trees

you said I was so
romantic

your eyes sparkled with mischief
and we both smiled

I was home to all your
waters
earth to the ebbs of
anxiety, of sadness, of longing
plants growing to the
flow of your dreams and
feelings and becoming

we are like an interdependent
organism, our family
me in a sea of you
earth in a house of water

how we cry
how we grow
how we thrive

were you afraid
to look at me
while we sang together
because we might
see each other?

or because you
didn't know
the words?

I always thought
you were the earth
in the changing seas of my childhood

you taught me how
to nest, how to be found

now in these years I see
that I too was earth
to your waters
a place to plant your roots
and dream

—*connected*

you are the evening light
cutting through the trees
mist on the rise of water
a hawk's wings piecing
the sky

you are the bright elegant moon
boldly singing with a smile
you are a field where wildflowers
play and at dusk, time becomes
like honey, and eyes can
see magic

if my parents were trees
they would be two oak seeds
blown downwind of their families

planted next to each other
roots not touching
until they are old enough
to find one another

they grow
branches entangled and
intermingled like lace against the sky
creating a canopy of life
above and below

who do you become
when you forget who you are?
and everyone
around you?

is it like being
reborn?

with the sight and
wonder and
magic of a child
in the old
wrinkly skin
of a life long-lived?

*I wake up
to the smell of rain
to birds, spinning their
spring songs through
the air*

*to the absence of you
beside me
to the fullness
of myself*

under your branches
I am showered with
flowers
they lay in the grass
like tiny fairy garlands
and on the pavement like
stars

how many ways
can I not say

I miss you
I love you
I hope something shifts
and we can be together?

thousands

thousands of ways while I
fold my clothes and
drive down the road

thousands

thousands of ways while
I close my eyes in the sun
and feel the ghost of
your arms around me

thousands

in the evolution
of a person
there is a stage
where everything is dark
and the damp earth
holds you
and the universe whispers
like I do, gently to my plants
my lips close to their
leaves:

> *you can grow*
> *you can grow*
> *you can grow*

*why do flowers grow
so slowly at the beginning
taking their sun in
lazily, stretching their
leaves with tiny
squeaks and sighs*

*perhaps they know
that time moves like honey
that there is no need
to rush the unfolding*

when I focus my eyes
I am like sunshine
through glass, magnified

I will pierce you
with my gaze

I will see you
and you will see
yourself
and when I soften
we both smile

there is healing in
softness
there is rest after truth

you can trust your voice.

mountains falling into me
like I am a river
and you are the avalanche.

you will crash.
and I will carry us home.

losing my voice
was a slow strangle

coming back to myself
is a flood.

I don't need you to believe me
anymore
to believe myself

you don't have to understand
to get it
to admit it

I know.
and the truth of it sings
in my bones

songs of pain
songs of grief
songs of rising

I gave birth to myself
in a bathtub under a skylight
with lotion in my hair

almost everyone thought
I was crazy
and I wondered, too

I thought I was pregnant
I could feel the time to
be born coming upon me
like a sudden storm drenching
everything I knew and saw and tasted
but that

it was time

to my surprise
there was no child, growing within me
but myself

ready to choose
ready to live
ready to be free

I thought magic would be
complicated, intricate, confusing

and it is
all of those things

but it is also
a sweet, simple knowing
a follow through of a breath
and a dream
the way salt cleanses in water
the way plants follow me
stuck to my feet, caught in
my hair, growing
growing despite it all

*you are all the yeses
written across the sky*

I'm a fool for loving you
but I do

I love you like
a flower gently and boldly
opening to the sun
joy spilling over
from every bright yellow petal

and don't you know
I am already yours?

*I'm learning how to breathe
again
to breathe without apology
without shame
to let the sounds and sighs
of my body free*

it changes everything

*today a bald eagle
swept the sky and
a fierce brown moth
snuggled into my blanket*

*how lovely
to pay attention*

I am starting to learn your body
the way a smile plays on your
face, the way your eyelashes
grow long and soft
how you put your lips
close to the place my neck
kisses my shoulders
and breathe

how you hold me with
fire in your palms
how your skin sings
when I trace you with my fingertips
I am starting to learn your body

every time I see you
it feels like goodbye

my heart holds on the longest

*I have come to every
point of breaking*

and I am made of light.

spiders weave their webs
between the peppers and tomatoes
bees come with dollops of
pollen collecting, shifting, becoming
on their hips

sunshine yellow flowers
transform into green orbs
growing round and firm with the
warm encouragement of
gravity and the gifts
of the sky

moon white flower stars
face the ground like lanterns
bells shifting, transforming into
peppers filled with fire

how brief the moment of the bee
how fleeting the life of the flower
how lovingly they give way to the
fruit becoming
how watchful the spiders

there is one dandelion
next to me this morning
petals like a golden mane
opening to a cloudy sky

how perfect she is
in such a simple act of
praise, a loving trust
in the way of becoming

to open is to be free.
to open is to surrender.
to open is to trust beauty.

I grew potato eyes
in my cupboard
and planted them hopefully

they have one hundred
leaves now

*the way your lips find
the curve of my neck*

maybe you came back into my life
to bring me home to myself
to help me see
and remember
what has made me
me, through all the
metamorphosis

maybe I was never meant to
love you, so easily, like a soft
sigh of relief to be found
by you, in you, with you

maybe we've lived our meant-
to be, already finishing before
we could land and root in
the possibility of waking up with
my head on your chest, of
creating some earth and fire magic

with our wildness
with our tenderness

I am earth
in a family of water

when something
happens to me
it shakes us all

maybe we love each other, again
maybe we circle the wide vast
galaxy of our wild wanderings
and find home in our
hearts, with our fingers
intertwined, and my cold
feet tucked under yours
because no socks in bed

maybe there's a future, or
another life where I get to be
lost in you, and you get to
be free in me
where we can learn
surrender and gasp
and breathe together

our love is like a weight between us

I don't think you deserve
this much poetry
this much room in my heart
this much waiting
this much wanting

do you know that I am
an artist with my love?

*you are a traveling forest fire
in the garden of my heart*

loving you is like loving a storm

I may be torn
I may be drenched
I may be devastated

I love you
I'm letting you go

—*the hardest things to say*

when I was 18, part of my
soul left my body
at the edge of the ocean
in a hospital bed
on the line of *I could stop breathing*
to the tune of *is this even worth it*

but I did not leave
my body

when I was 27, my soul
flew back to myself
surrounded with snow
seeing visions, my body distorting
crashing into fears
lighting ever candle
and dancing until I could
sing again

and what a homecoming it has been

when I was a child
my parents bought me a suitcase

I did not realize
they were giving me
wings

I did not realize
written in the fabric of the little
black case were the
words, over and over

you are free
you are free
you are free

we keep meeting each other
across time
coming face to face
again and again
our energies swelling
to one another
weaving stars across
the universe
in our wake

we were lovers
in some past life

how we've traveled
worlds
to be together

how I can feel the
stars in your skin

how I can see the
future in your eyes

we've found each other
before

I have walked this
cosmos with you

I have whispered
the name of your heart
in worship, in love
in friendship, in song
and written you like poetry
with starlight on the sky

how lucky I am
to find you again

how you already know me

I am earth
but you have shown me
how to move in waves

that change requires movement
transformation begs for surrender
rebirth comes with openness

I am better for your wisdom.

the sky is heavy with you today
with the waters of my
family, those who birthed me
and those who chose me

I feel your magic like
rich chocolate cake
like the texture of a deep
breath of almost rain dusk air
like all the times you've held me
and said *it's going to be ok*

you taught me
that everything is always
changing

that to shift
is to be alive

and you rose up
out of the ocean
and you were free

I was raised in a house of water.

www.ingramcontent.com/pod-product-compliance
Lightning Source LLC
Chambersburg PA
CBHW030852170426
43193CB00009BA/583